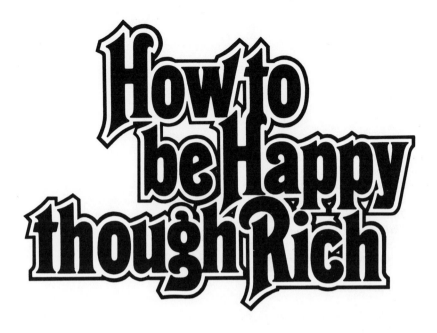

How to be Happy though Rich

A book every poor person should read!

Peter J. Daniels

THE HOUSE OF TABOR

Other Titles by Peter J. Daniels:
How To Reach Your Life Goals
How To Be Motivated All The Time
How To Have The Awesome Power Of Public Speaking
How To Handle A Major Crisis
Miss Phillips You Were Wrong
Global Survey Into Multi-Level Marketing
How To Create Your Own Dynamic Mission Statement That Works

Tutorial programs:
Destiny
How To Get More Done And Have Time Left Over

All correspondence to:
World Centre for Entrepreneurial Studies
38-40 Carrington Street, Adelaide, South Australia 5000
Telephone: (08) 8231 0111   Facsimile (08) 8211 8423

How To Be Happy Though Rich
Copyright © 1984 by Peter J. Daniels
National Library of Australia card number
and ISBN 0 949330 03 5

Acknowledgement
To Peter and Erica Haran
for valued assistance in compiling this book.

Printed and bound in Australia
by Gillingham Printers of Adelaide, South Australia.

Published by

World Centre for Entrepreneurial Studies
38-40 Carrington Street, Adelaide, South Australia 5000
Telephone: 61-8-8231 0111   Facsimile: 61-8-8211 8423

Dedicated to
W. Clement Stone
my mentor and friend
who understands
the contents of this book
better than anyone
I know

Contents

FOREWORD

Can a Christian be wealthy? Can a Christian strive and succeed in the business world, accrue money and still be in line with the basic Biblical teaching on money and material wealth? Peter Daniels believes he can.

Millionaire land developer Peter Daniels attempts to address and come to grips with the questions which face many Christians in today's materialistic and success-orientated society.

In this book, he looks at the influence of money and the pursuit of wealth within the parameters of a Christian walk. He is a man sufficiently qualified to write on the subject.

Coming from a broken home, Peter quit school at the age of 14, branded by his teacher as an illiterate "who would never amount to anything."

A messenger boy . . . a cleaner . . . a milk vendor . . . a factory hand, the young Peter Daniels tried it all, eventually becoming a bricklayer in an attempt to break into the building industry.

In 1959 his life changed forever. Along with his wife, Robina, he attended a Billy Graham Crusade and gave his life to Christ.

A realisation hit the young battler that if all men were equal before God, then no-one need look down on him as a no-hoper anymore. "I'm the son of a King!" said Peter—a motto since printed on the back of his Rolls Royce.

Today, he claims Christ is his motivator. He earns to spend and employ others in furthering the Word of God. The vehicle for his earning power is a business and property development company with interests in Australia and South East Asia. But his approach to making and spending money is what some would call unique among the business community—a fact he attempts to clarify in this book.

He probes and evaluates wealth and its effects on the Christian and the non-Christian. He looks at wealth as a power base, as an influence on others, and as a tool in the hands of the devoted Christian. He explores society's attitudes towards those with wealth and how the Christian making and distributing money should treat criticism.

"A Christian should control his money—his money should never control him", Peter explains.

As well as running his business and working with his local church, Peter is currently a representative on many Australian and international Christian organisations. They include the Robert Schuller Ministries, Youth For Christ (Australia), Youth For Christ International and the Haggai Institute for Advanced Leadership Training. As a moral campaigner he founded the Festival of Light.

As well as being a speaker of international renown, he is the epitome of the successful businessman, although in his walk with Christ and in his business ventures he freely admits to his failings and shortcomings as well as his success.

But throughout his rags-to-riches story, he maintains, "Christ is my life, I am nothing without Him."

Reading how a Christian deals with wealth is reading the Peter Daniels story.

Peter Haran,
Journalist

LIFE IS NOT A DRESS REHEARSAL

Life is not a dress rehearsal,
  in a kaleidoscope parade,
it's a time of guts and thinking,
  it is honour unafraid.

Life is not a dress rehearsal,
  that fools and jesters crave;
it is helping, winning, serving,
  it is finding better ways.

Life is not a dress rehearsal—
  it's opportunity and chance;
it is maker of the man,
  not a thing of circumstance.

Life is not a dress rehearsal—
  every day is opening night.
Now's the time to reach the goals,
  now's the time to stand and fight.

Life is not a dress rehearsal,
  so keep your stars in sight;
it's God's good gift of grace—
  and it's for you to keep it right.

Life is not a dress rehearsal
  with excuses, props and paint—
it's time to show them what you are—
  a sinner or a saint?

Life is not a dress rehearsal,
  it's success within your grasp;
it's your destiny, your purpose,
  and the sands of time move fast.

Life is not a dress rehearsal,
   never compromise the thought;
it's overcoming, keep on running—
   your dreams will soon be bought!

Life is not a dress rehearsal;
   press on upwards to the heights;
on the mountain top you'll give it—
   the performance of your life!

Peter Daniels

CHAPTER ONE

Wealth Is Relative

Wherever money is concerned, we always tend to measure ourselves against someone who has much more rather than someone who has much less!

CHAPTER ONE

Wealth Is Relative

From time to time I receive anonymous letters and hear through "back door critics" what I should do with my money, and how I should live my life. I occasionally think of how I would like to meet my unknown critics, sceptics and advisers and remind them that all wealth is relative. Many well-meaning, but fuzzy-thinking, people are often eager to place restrictions on others who are richer than they.

Biblical truths—plus the critics' own suggested principles and opinions, which they feel are applicable to people with wealth—are in fact usually more applicable to themselves.

They need to be aware of the fact that the same restrictions, and obligations, must bind their lives, too, if sincerity is to be recognised at all.

Relativity was driven home to me by, of all people, the Beatles. During the 60's the music scene of the world was caught up with "Beatle Mania". In many cases the young musicians from Liverpool captivated the old as well as the young with their new style and beat of music. Wherever they went, the Beatles

created traffic jams, unprecedented box office sell-outs
and incredible record sales, within a very short space
of time, many other groups appeared, copying their
appearance and style.

My first encounter of "Beatle Mania" was on my
television screen, where I saw them surrounded by a
screaming crowd outside a concert hall. Then they
were shown performing in a style and sound which
was very different. That style and sound has now
become a part of entertainment history.

It wasn't the crowds, or even the music that arrested
my attention so vividly that day . . . it was the
appearance of the four young men. Although they
were expensively dressed, they wore their clothes
sloppily and behaved badly. They certainly needed a
hair cut!

That first contact with the Beatles left an indelible
impression on my mind. I had forgotten the incident
until recently, when I was sitting relaxed in my lounge,
watching television. During the particular programme I was viewing, they were showing news flash
backs. Suddenly, the same news clip I had seen so
many years before came on the screen. Instantly I
thought, as I looked at the four young men, how clean
cut they looked, and how reserved the music was . . .
until I remembered that these were the same young
men who had shocked me, and whom I had criticized
so many years before! In the 60's, to many of those
in my generation, the Beatles were scruffy, uncouth,
and loud . . . and yet today they are considered by
some as being almost classical!

Looking back, although it is still not my kind of
musical scene, I have to admit that music, and styles
of presentation of music, are relative.

We often tend to relate ourselves against others and
vice versa. In discussion about health, for instance we
compare ourselves favourably or unfavourably with

other people's physical conditions. We relate moods, tastes, likes and dislikes against the climate of the prevailing situation. But what seems to escape our blinkered eyes and our protected egos, is that we should be relating ourselves against what we call in business "the bottom line". In other words, some things may be relative to the situation as a matter of expediency or convenience. But on the other hand, what about the overall principle and our personal relationship and lifestyle to that principle?

Wherever money is concerned, we always tend to measure ourselves against someone who has much more, rather than someone who has much less! We fail to consider the relative difference from where we are against those who are pitifully poor; and we fail to relate *that* against where we are now and how far we can go to stretch ourselves in at least an effort to meet the urgency and magnitude of the need.

The point that I am making is simply this ... it doesn't matter whether you are a labourer, a technician, an executive, a company director, a housewife, or unemployed and on welfare benefits. *You are rich* compared with those who are disadvantaged by real poverty and famine or those war-torn refugees who represent the untold millions of this world for whom Christ died. The argument for your disadvantaged position, whether it is imposed by others or by yourself, is a very poor argument against such overwhelming, universal need.

It is very convenient to argue exclusively against the millionaire to support a position of personal philosophy and economy. But it is a very different picture when the argument is fully explored and expanded to include the other end of the scale. Now the critic is seen as the object of criticism! And because of our inability or unwillingness to recognize that comparison with those who are starving, homeless and without human hope, although *we are rich* beyond measure, we are sterile in our compassion and action.

Wealth is relative when you consider that God looks not on the various areas of the world in isolation, but sees the world as a whole, and that the principles of work, effort, caring and giving apply to all, and cannot be sectionalized to suit the convenience of some. They must apply more stringently to those in better economic positions, however more slightly than others, irrespective of geographical boundaries.

Just imagine if you will, that you are sitting at home, watching television, and seeing the horror of war, or experiencing shock at the sight of death by starvation. A tear may form in your eye, and you may not even be able to eat your evening meal because of your concern. You are upset and you use the all-familiar expression, "Why doesn't someone do something about it?" Or maybe you are a highly spiritual person and you drop to the floor on your knees and pray that God will convict someone rich or powerful and send him to help. You may even become practical and ask that the church you attend do something.

You may go even further and examine your own resources. You may realise that you're not in a very good position relative to your neighbour, but you do send a gift anyway, and then you feel better.

During that evaluation it is futile to examine ourselves by our own standards, or even by the standards of our neighbour. It is even pseudo-rational to measure from our national average as a point of reference.

We need to measure ourselves against the suffering and afflicted, realizing that against that situation *we are rich* and that is why *all wealth* is relative!

Why God has allowed us to be born in this particular space of time is something that remains a mystery, but nevertheless, it is real and dynamic and full of personal obligation.

Wealth is relative, and our response in respect to the principle of God is that we share, not on the basis of what others who are better equipped, or lesser equipped, than ourselves are doing, but *on the basis of how we are individually blessed compared to the intensity of the need*.

Many years ago when I was at a crisis point in my business and my creditors were crowding in, sales were down, opportunities were minimal and everything looked black, I went to my bank manager to try and obtain more funds.

He glared at me suspiciously and took out the file covering all of my previous transactions with the bank. He went through them meticulously and as he went through page after page, I saw his head shaking from side to side and heard him sighing as if in great pain. Finally he looked up and said, "Mr. Daniels, you have all the money that the bank can advance you against the minimum assets and potential you have".

Whilst I did not expect the red carpet welcome or a huge amount of money, I was stunned at the response. I knew that unless I got the money I needed, my business would collapse.

Then suddenly I thought with some insight as to my true wealth. I looked at my bank manager, who was in his late fifties, unmarried and lonely. I told him that I had other assets far in excess of those that were written in my file handled by the bank. He looked up with a start and asked if I had been holding out on the bank! I said, "You have not taken careful note of the assets that I have". He asked me to identify them. I slammed my hand down on his desk. I said, "One wife, worth at least one million dollars, three children worth at least one million dollars each". Finally, I looked at him and said, "For those kinds of assets are you trying to tell me I can't have the money I want to salvage my business?"

He was very quiet for a while and I know, from conversations I had with him later, that although he was quite a wealthy man outside of the bank he saw his own wealth as relative alongside of my obvious wealth. He gave me the funds I required!

I believe with all my heart that it is a master stroke of Satan to get our minds off our own relative blessedness, and our commitment of service, on to someone or something else that will destroy our effectiveness, and stifle our total commitment. The millionaire may be one hundred times more wealthy than you and it is very easy to philosophize, criticize and rationalize against that protected perspective. On the other hand, consider that *you* are one hundred times more wealthy than others in this world! Now you are in a goldfish bowl with every eye looking in on you, examining your lifestyle! In that situation, you can be assured that the disadvantaged people of the world would have a very good argument against your unwillingness to share your relative wealth with them.

You may be a teenager in your first job, or newly-married with heavy commitments, or middle-aged and facing increased family responsibilities and expense, or even unemployed or on a pension. Or, by opportunity and obedience, God may have blessed you with unusual wealth. No matter who you are, you are still wealthy—enormously wealthy—relative to the disadvantaged of other countries.

To all of us, without compromise, loop-holes or option, the principles of the Bible apply.

The seriousness of recognizing our relative position, not in relationship with our peers, but in relationship with other people's needs, must always remain the real spiritual acid test.

CHAPTER TWO

Wealth Is Commitment

Every morning I wake up in debt to the needs of others, and I know that each day, each week and each year I must pay that debt so that others can be called to different spheres of service . . .

CHAPTER TWO

Wealth Is Commitment

People generally do not like to make a commitment. They will avoid it by pseudo-virtue with such a statement as, "I don't want to make a commitment to myself and then break it". If you disagree with this, you need to ask several people to make a medium or long term commitment that could be monitored and displayed. Better still, maybe *you* could make a public medium or long term commitment yourself, by setting some goal that will cause your life to expand, and thereby make yourself more measurably productive (e.g. to reduce weight or learn a verse from the Bible each week).

You may react by saying, "I will make a commitment for something, but I do not want anyone else to know about it". In other words, it is a private commitment so that you don't want to boast about it to others. But what if you could do it without boasting? What if it was just some simple statement of fact like, "By a certain date, six months from now, I will have lost four kilograms", or, "By a certain date one year from now, I will have read the Bible through completely to enhance my biblical knowledge", or, "I will run two kilometres every day, without missing a single day, to keep fit".

I dare you! Pin it up where your friends can see it and produce a visible record of your progress. A hard decision to make? . . . Difficult to follow through? . . . Of course it is! Because it is easier to fall back than to press ahead. If we tell only ourselves, then we can easily hide our failures. Very few of us are prepared to make our lives transparent enough for scrutiny.

Most people find it easy to renege on a commitment that they have made only to themselves; but pushing forward, and achieving results publicly is a commitment.

It is interesting to contemplate that all Christians rejoice as they see people making a commitment and giving their lives to Christ. Many, like my own commitment, and that of my wife, were made at a Billy Graham crusade meeting all within the space of an hour or two. We made a commitment for *life*.

Yet contrast that if you will, against a commitment to improve your financial position, health or spiritual accountability, and you suddenly get a large dose of "excusiology", "I must not rush" . . . "I'm not sure if it is right just now" . . . "Maybe that is not God's plan" . . .

When the truth is known, in many cases, it simply requires too much effort or we are afraid to expose ourselves to the risk of failure.

We need to be reminded that God is committed to our development, and that the reservation is always on our part. Very often we expect God to do for us, what we are just *too lazy* to do for ourselves.

Some time ago, as I was preparing to go out for the evening, the phone rang, and the conversation started in the usual way when someone calls at our home or office for help. "Mr. Daniels?" said the caller, "you don't know me but . . ." and then his voice broke into a whimper as he said, "I have been a Christian for fifteen years. I am desperate. I feel as if my life is wasting away. Nothing is happening. God hasn't given me a special task or direction, and after all these years of waiting, I still have no idea what God's will is for my life."

Here I was, waiting to go out to keep another commitment with only limited time at my disposal, and someone on the other end of the phone was in a distressing situation. My caller went on to expose the hurt, the disappointment and the discouragement which was overwhelming him.

After some time I had to interrupt him to ask a question. "On the basis of the inactive life that you have just described to me, and your non-demanding job, what have you been doing in the last fifteen years to equip yourself for the service that you so eagerly claim you want? Have you done, for instance, a course on public speaking? Studied effective and corporate management? Computer programming? Or fundamental accountancy? . . .", I continued to run off a long list until he interrupted me with an urgent tone in his voice saying, "No! No! I've done none of those!"

I said rather firmly, "Are you then expecting God to use you in areas where you have neither equipped yourself to do the job, nor demonstrated any commitment to service?" In defence he replied that he couldn't move until he knew for sure what was God's will. I hastily reminded him that the Bible says, "God's will is that none should perish", and could it be that, if he became involved in a soul-winning ministry, he would be within the circumference of God's will? I also reminded him of Abraham Lincoln who said, "I will study and prepare, and my opportunity will come."

Some months later after I had addressed a meeting, a man approached me and identified himself as my anxious caller. He told me that he was experiencing the thrill, the satisfaction and the pressure of commitment, as he had undertaken study, and given of himself through a very real, measurable commitment.

When looking at part or full-time Christian service, consideration is often given to pastoral, counselling, mission field and youth work. Further extensions go into areas of music, linguistics, mass media and other conventional and not so conventional areas of involvement. But how many Christians consider being called into the *service* of wealth? Now it may be a shock for you to consider wealth as a *calling* . . . but stay with me as I develop it further.

Many years ago when I was challenged by God to go into business, become successful and thus give a lifetime to success, I, too, reacted against it. It was easy to react, particularly in my position, without status, learning or money. And I would argue to myself and seek scriptural reference to thwart the positive aspects of such a calling. Yet, contrary to that, I saw the tremendous need in the areas of finance, influence and leadership within the Christian church as being desperate beyond measure. I had to consider questions such as, "What would others think if I even suggested such a call? Would those closest to me understand? What can I expect of Christian peers at that level? And if so . . . where are they? What personal equipment do I possess for such a goal? Can I find supporting scriptures to guide me?"

As I continued in prayer, not knowing how to pray in a situation like this, and as I read about the promises of prosperity to Abraham and others, I came to grips with the fact that Jesus did indeed seek out prosperous men like Zacchaeus, Matthew, Joseph of Arimathea, and Paul. As they came face to face with the King of kings, they *gave their money away to bless others.*

As the response to "the call" to become wealthy

weighed upon me, I tended to become a parade watcher on the local church scene, observing that it was easier to talk about and get people involved in singing, attending worship, teaching and praying, but the mere mention of financial commitment, was like pulling a revolver in a bank . . . all hands went up and nobody moved!

It was only a limited few who went to the challenge meetings to give financial support, and fewer still who made the financial commitment. I decided to look at it from a different perspective by asking my Christian friends and acquaintances about their giving programme, only to receive blank stares, hostile remarks, or weak excuses.

It was during that enquiry, however, that I met the dedicated givers who seemed to be released in a very special way that was difficult for me to fully comprehend. The lives and attitudes of these people seemed to have a *love commitment of the will* that was to affect me from then on.

By this time I was convinced that with God's help and guidance, I would commit myself to a lifetime task. Not for a moment, did I realise the magnitude of the undertaking in personal discipline alone. I was to understand later, in no small measure, Paul's words when he said, "I will pummel my body into submission" (1 Cor. 9:27). As I studied and experimented, I failed, only to fail again, and again. Sometimes, exhausted in body, mind and spirit, I had to front up again, succeed in a mediocre way, and fail again. I couldn't collect my ideas together or articulate them to other people, and my financial management was in chaos.

I was to be mis-understood, laughed at, mis-interpreted, and even avoided. During one five year period I could not put a foot right, and no-one was interested in hearing me speak in public, even though I was practising daily. Because of my financial and physical condition, it was suggested that I give up, but the commitment that God had burnt into my heart stood fast, and I would reply, "God is dealing with me, and only He knows how stubborn I am, and how much I need the discipline".

During the five year period, I literally wore out a Bible, sometimes reading well into the night, seeking out principles of living. It was through those years I learnt that to become wealthy requires an incredible commitment. I was to learn later, that wealth involved many other commitments, too.

Many people have commitments on hire-purchase for television sets, refrigerators, and motor cars, and these debts are a commitment that must be met on a weekly or monthly basis. Consider if you will, a call from God to wealth. It means that after learning in some measure how to create wealth, that wealth is *always* totally committed, and as it is increased, so is the commitment to give increased. Every morning, when I wake up, I know I have to create wealth for the purpose of giving it away to others so that they can fulfil their call in the area that God has committed them to. Every day the debt to them grows.

Every morning I wake up in debt to the needs of others, and I know that each day, each week, and each year, I must pay that debt so that others can be called to different spheres of service. Yes . . . wealth may bring the prestige and recognition of the crowds, but deep in the heart, it is commitment.

I would like to see in my lifetime if there are any boundaries in Luke 6:38 which says, "Give and it will be given to you. A good measure, pressed down, shaken together and running over . . . For with the measure you use, it will be measured to you." Remember always . . . it is the educated who can help the uneducated, and the healthy who can assist the sick. Likewise, only the rich can help the poor. If you want to be happy though rich, make a commitment to learn daily to give your money away . . . accept a love debt! (Romans 13:8).

CHAPTER THREE

Wealth Is Responsibility

Wealth has a responsibility towards those of this world who are disadvantaged mentally, physically, spiritually or geographically by circumstances beyond their control . . .

CHAPTER THREE

Wealth Is Responsibility

Some years ago a very wealthy industrialist was preparing to retire and hand over the ownership and management of the organization he had founded 50 years earlier to his only son. The son was understandably elated. He knew more than anyone else of the tremendous wealth involved, and the thought of eventually selling out and enjoying the so called "good life" was paramount in his mind.

As the preparation for the transfer came closer to reality, the father, in his wisdom, spent the eve of the actual happening with his son in order to re-affirm the events of the coming day, to share some thoughts and give some advice.

The father/son relationship had always been good, and in that climate of mutual trust and affection, the father shared with his son some of the disappointments, heartaches and joys that he had experienced over the past 50 years, working with the staff and developing projects. Sometimes this required working late into the night. But there was always a spirit of co-operation and mutual respect between the management and staff.

The father talked about the organization's beginnings when he worked shoulder to shoulder with his employees and there was a real feeling of comradeship. He explained to his son that he knew the names of the wives and the children, and even the grandchildren and at times they shared their problems and joys; they dreamed together, and in times of personal tragedies, wept together. "Some of the people who started with me in the beginning," said the father, "are still working for me today. Others, including their sons and daughters, and even grand-children are working for us today in this organization. Although it is a huge company with many facets of production and marketing, I still know many of them by their first names."

There was a deep silence as if the father wanted the weight of those words to sink into his son's mind, and then he added. "There will be no work for the staff tomorrow morning, because after the handing over ceremony, the official speeches and signing of documents, I have arranged for the complete staff to stand in a long line, and I will take you down that line and introduce you to each person as the new president of this giant organization. And my son," his father continued, "as I introduce you to them in your new position of power and wealth I want you to take each hand and hold it firmly and look deeply into each person's eyes. As you hold their hands, repeat continually to yourself as you go down the line, with every person, 'I am responsible for you . . . I am responsible for you . . . I am responsible for you . . . I am responsible for you . . . .'."

What happened to the son, of course, was a dramatic realisation that *wealth is responsibility.*

The principles of responsibility in respect to wealth must apply to us all. Whether we have little or much, the principle of responsibility still stands.

A further responsibility comes from living in a country that has obvious wealth, where we must stretch ourselves to participate in its acquisition. A young man once confessed to me he had continually criticized those who were wealthier than himself, until he reached a point of total commitment in his life. It was then that he realised that he was afraid to acquire wealth because of the responsibilities it brought. His fear was that he would be swept away with its implications and indulgences. He seemed to understand at that point that *wealth is responsibility*.

Wealth is responsibility, because you have an option in wealth to withhold it and become withdrawn, greedy, and selfish; or to accept it as a grand opportunity to demonstrate that a Christian is prepared to grasp opportunities to create jobs, and to provide products and services which will enhance life. It, in turn, places more responsibility on your shoulders to keep people employed, to provide salaries and good conditions, and to maintain a caring attitude for those who entrust their working life to you.

Wealth, with its responsibility, holds a commitment to expand skills, to expand one's ability to grow and to continue to venture into new fields to provide more wealth, and in turn, more opportunities for others.

You are not so much dealing with money, but with purchased goods and time that represent the life and livelihood of other human beings. Wealth has a responsibility towards those of this world who are disadvantaged mentally, physically, spiritually or geographically by circumstances beyond their control. Such a responsibility can only be discharged very often by goods and services such as food, machinery, and medical help which can only be obtained by hard cash.

Wealth has additional responsibilities of leadership, because if one becomes wealthy, then the commitment is a commitment to be in the "people business"

and in dealing with people, the principle clearly
emerges that if you cannot, or will not, act as a leader
in guiding, encouraging and building people, you in
turn cannot grow.

But getting back to the fundamental fact that wealth
is responsibility, the question must be asked, "How
far must my responsibility go in respect to *distributing*
that wealth?".

My own fundamentals are simple. Firstly, I just
accept the fact that *I own nothing, and that all I have
is a gift from God and entrusted to me.*

Secondly, I accept the principle of *tithing ten per cent
of my personal income* to my local church.

Thirdly, I accept the principle of *a double tithe, plus
gifts and offerings* (Deut. 12:4–7). These are given
according to personal conscience and the direction of
the Holy Spirit, (and this, I might add, often leads one
into a commitment of faith which may become a debt
against future earning expectations!).

You may even find that you have to adjust your
financial goals to meet a need, which may mean a
greater personal commitment in your life. I accept
that once a person does give, whether under the direct
leadership of God, or out of a reasoned decision, that
person's own responsibility ends. And to give expecting or requiring some form of return is *trading*, not
giving. To expect a position of authority because of a
gift is a means of buying power, and not a total giving
commitment.

It is ludicrous to accept that the government, the
church, or some other personal organization should
shoulder the responsibility of helping others without
accepting the responsibility to the individual . . . *you*.
The person who has no sense of responsibility will not
generally change because of inherited wealth. In fact,
some studies have been undertaken with regard to
people who have won enormous sums of money in

lotteries, or by unexpected means, such as an inheritance, only to find out a few years later that it was all gone and nothing worthwhile had been accomplished, and very little, if anything, remained. The general rule is, if you are irresponsible with little, you will not be responsible with much (Luke 19:17).

I am not suggesting, for one moment, that all wealthy people accept the responsibility of wealth in a humane and kindly way. There are some who personally want more and more wealth, not caring who they hurt or what they do to get it. What I am suggesting is, that if you want to be "happy though rich", you need to be responsible with your wealth to those around you. Although people's time can be purchased with money, remember you do not own the person, God does. Although wealth can be used for evil purposes, it can also be used to glorify God, and to do good.

The burning questions are, "How much should you keep for yourself?" and "What sort of lifestyle should you adopt?". The answers to those questions are obviously personal ones.

John the Baptist was called for a specific purpose, and his lifestyle in the wilderness was an integral part of that call. David was called to kingship, and *his* lifestyle was in keeping with that call. My life and lifestyle is also relative to God's call. The over-riding conviction is that I am only a trustee of the wealth God has given me. Naturally, wealth may take you around the world and into the high echelons of government, and commercial enterprise, where etiquette requires the giving of hospitality and entertaining which, to be fair, must be in line with hospitality received. But also it must always be consistent with biblical principles.

CHAPTER FOUR

Wealth Is Accountability

Wealth and money are part of the significant measure of your life, because if you trade an hour of your time for a pittance, then you have measured the value of your life for that period . . .

CHAPTER FOUR

Wealth Is Accountability

There seems to be (in Christian circles) a reluctance to be accountable. We tend to spend money, time and talent, very often without paying any heed to accountability, and reckoning of good sense. Let me explain further. The catch-phrase in many Christian enterprises, whether it be for growth, evangelism, or teaching, after total effort and money has been spent and very little results forthcoming, is, "We must not be discouraged or disappointed because if it affects the life of one single person, it was worth it." I am sure that all Christians, regardless of their denominational tag have heard something like that. After such a comment most people feel that any word to the contrary is either unwelcome or unspiritual!

We need to be careful not to lull ourselves into a feeling of achievement without measurement, which is a dangerous practice to follow.

How would you feel, for instance, if your children related that to their school work? Or, would you consider that your favourite football team was measuring up if they did not kick one goal on a grand final match but came back to you, the supporter, and said, "Don't be discouraged because we didn't kick any goals. Please accept that just by our being here and running around the field today, we at least made the game possible". Ridiculous? Of course it is!

But how often do we prepare unwisely, operate inefficiently, and follow through negligently in Christian work or service, and then let ourselves off the hook when nothing is achieved, instead of measuring our effectiveness against effort *plus* spiritual enhancement!

From time to time, I am called upon by pastors to counsel Christians who have gone into business and failed. Many of these good people have started with nothing more than a dream, and on that dream they have mortgaged their house, and gone into heavy debt to begin a business venture. In most cases, I have found that the people in question had a great desire to serve God in the area of providing finance. But in most cases, I have also found that they were ill equipped to handle normal finance, let alone understand the commercial laws of business. In most cases, they knew almost nothing about business principles generally, let alone the speciality in which they decided to operate. Very often no market studies were undertaken, no budgets prepared, no feasibility studies on sales or cash flow made, no examination into overheads carried out, or a break-even figure calculated. There was however, a genuine, honest keenness to succeed. At their lowest ebb they must wonder if God had forgotten them! Surely not!

What was overlooked was, "Wealth is accountability". Yet there is a reluctance not only by Christians, but by people in many areas of life, to be involved in any kind of measurement that can enhance the possibilities of success. The comment I often hear is, "I failed because I was too honest," or, "You can't succeed if you are honest."

The implication of course, is that all successful

people are *dishonest*, I am sure that very few people would accept that assumption. What I believe many Christians are trying to say is, "If I decide to honour my Christian commitment by going into business to give, or for any other reason, then I don't want to have to face up to measurement."

The attitude amongst Christians today is that they just want to "jog along" in business without competition, pressure or accountability! I have to disagree with that attitude, and suggest that the story of the talents in the Bible (Matt. 25) disagrees with it also. In fact, almost every area of human existence disagrees with it. In musical notation we use middle C as a reference point even for great symphonies. Greenwich Mean Time is used for world time zones to keep our airlines, business and sport accurate. Vitamins and minerals in our food, and exercise, will soon show the measurement of our physical well-being. Soil is measured by what it can produce to enhance life. Because we live in a country of abundance and opportunity we must therefore be prepared to put up our lives for scrutiny. As Christians and as loyal citizens of our country we must measure ourselves against the national wealth and the relative opportunities within the system to acquire wealth and accept the cold hard facts of the results of such an acquisition.

It seems to me, that it is fashionable to accept a protected sort of poverty in our Christian circles as a badge of honour, instead of using it as a catalyst for challenge.

If we Christians are unwilling to accept a measurement on our wealth performance, then I say carefully, but deliberately, that we are delinquent in our Christian responsibility. We are no example to our fellow citizens, nor do we show true responsibility to those who are disadvantaged both in our country and in other countries.

You may want to get off the hook by using the analogy, "I heard of a man who was wealthy and his wife and children hated him. He had fears, hang-ups and personal problems which were almost insurmountable." I am sure there are those people around, but my experience has been that the rich are able to handle the problems better, if they have them, because they can afford better help! Poor people have just as many, and often more problems, than those wealthier than themselves. Many of them are caused by their low economic positions, and they often remain in the problem situation because of poor teaching, negative attitudes, as well as their low economic status.

Society, whether we like it or not, has *chosen* wealth as a measurement, and we have accepted it, if we are using money for any purpose. You are paid a wage relative to the work you do. If you are in business, you are receiving remuneration for services or goods you supply. You are paid by a measurement taken from the market place, against other people who are prepared to compete on the same basis. If we were to accept the pure communistic viewpoint that all people be paid the same amount, it would still mean that it would require a measurement to be made against needs. Even in strong communist countries, there are those who are measured higher up the scale in money benefits or special privileges, by measurement of worth of their performance.

Wealth and money are part of the significant measure of your life, because if you trade an hour of your time for a pittance, then you have measured the value of your life for that period accordingly, and that reflects a "wealth measurement".

Obviously, there are many things that money can *never* buy, such as the respect and love of your family, but I am speaking in this book to those people who have committed their lives to Christ and accept the

Biblical principles as final.

How do you evaluate a person who tells his family that he loves them and is unwilling to stretch to provide adequately for them? I heard about a man who found it difficult to manage on unemployment benefits, and who claimed he wanted to be a better provider for his family. I was sympathetic, and seeking more information, I decided to visit his home to see what could be done to help.

The man I met was about 40, big, strong and anxiously waiting for whatever could be done to help him. He explained the limiting factors of the unemployment cheque, and the hopelessness of just waiting with nothing to do. As we talked, I looked out of the window and saw a very large back yard with weeds standing knee high. I asked him if he would accept a position as a part-time gardener with no tax paid on the income, and he revelled at the unexpected opportunity. I told him I would provide tools, seed and equipment for him to garden his own back yard where he could work and provide probably all of the vegetables for his family food needs. Furthermore he would be able to grow additional items suitable for chicken feed in exchange for eggs with the man down the road.

He was immediately downcast and said that he didn't want to do that. Then I asked him, "What would you like to do if there were no limitations?" He mentioned a field of industry for which he had very little knowledge, and I replied, "I have great news for you. We have in our city, one of the finest libraries in the world. Why don't you spend several hours a day studying the area of employment you want, and then offer your services free of charge for two weeks to a possible employer, so that he can measure your worth." Well . . . I was talking to deaf ears. What the man wanted was life without measurement or accountability.

If you live in a community and you want to be "salt" and thus flavour that community with a Christian viewpoint, you need a platform from which people will be anxious to hear you speak. What better platform could you have, than a family and church life that is sound, supported by your own demonstrated ability to be measured on the economic board of achievement? What better platform could you have than to have a good credit rating? Wealth obtained by an individual in a prosperous country says to the world at large, "I will accept that God has placed me in a unique position in the world, geographically speaking, and I have used that opportunity wisely and well in gratitude and as an act of obedience to that positioning by God".

Wealth must be a measurement of Christian service if we live in a prosperous country of opportunity. Therefore we must be accountable as to its acquisition, expansion and distribution.

Wealth Is Leadership

If you are a Christian, you are leader elect; if you are not leading, you are in fact a leader in abdication or self-imposed exile . . .

CHAPTER FIVE

Wealth Is
Leadership

When we look at the volume of books, the numbers of seminars, sermons and talks on leadership, we have to be arrested by the questions: Where *are* the leaders, and why aren't there *more* of them?

I think the answer lies somewhere within the ranks of the followers, because every leader was once a follower, and that is where leaders come from.

The need for leaders has always been evident, and the absence of them has always been just as evident. Just look at recent history where times and events are blotted by the blood of followers without leaders.

In reality there should be no scarcity of leaders, particularly among Christians, because their encompassing call and life challenge is to be a *light*, which, in its simplest and highest form, gives direction and prevents stumbling. Christians are also to be *salt*, which by its very nature can preserve and penetrate. Leadership to a Christian is not optional, it is mandatory.

If you are a Christian, you are a leader elect; and if you are not leading, you are in fact a leader in abdication or self-imposed exile.

Leadership is a directional compass set on a pre-determined course for others to follow, as well as a confidence anchor for timid ships to cling to.

You can be a leader in the area of your vocation, by being the best in your field. You can be a leader in sports, academics or home life. You can be a student, a pensioner, or a gardener. You can be in bereavement or in achievement. Whatever your circumstances, you can show others the best God-given way to handle, and excel in, every situation.

A leader, among other things, has always been a person who can create, recognize, motivate, initiate and inspire. The causes to hold aloft are always there, but unfortunately there are too few who are prepared to meet and deal with the causes. Those who want more effective leadership must continually ask themselves the question, "Am I an effective follower in the area of loyalty and willingness to work for a cause?" In a sense we are all followers because there is no human who has either the capacity or ability to lead in all areas.

Wealth leadership has been a particularly neglected area of service for Christians. Wealth leaders were extremely evident in biblical times—Abraham, David, Solomon, Job (after he passed the test) and of course Joseph of Arimathea, who supplied the tomb for the temporary burial of the Lord Himself. As a matter of fact, financial and material rewards throughout biblical history were presented by God for obedience, and removed for lack of obedience. Remember that a number of disciples had their own businesses, and include, too, the earthly father of Jesus, who operated a carpentry shop within the free enterprise system.

Wealth entails leadership more for a Christian than anyone else, simply because of the scriptural obligations surrounding a believer's life.

Firstly, all riches must be obtained honestly and

within the confines of scriptural liberty. Secondly, tithes and offerings must be proportional to income. Thirdly, people you work with or those who work for you, must be dealt with under better conditions than the world may expect. Fourthly, in the light of all that, you have to make a profit and build a wealth base. And, finally, above all else, is the mercy commitment factor that may mean complete disposal of your wealth at any given time.

The conditions and perimeters for Christian wealth are so *spartan* as to make the most determined applicant run in fear or retreat when the battle lines are drawn. Loose catch phrases such as, "I could never succeed in business because I am too honest", indicate the shallowness of thinking by some people who in that context are suggesting that all business people are corrupt, and all non-business people (particularly the person making the comment!) are pure.

The facts are clear that it takes ability and stickability to create wealth, and there are additional Biblical ingredients for the Christian. It takes no ability to stand on the sidelines and dream or condemn in self-imposed ignorance.

I remember an occasion when I returned to my office, and as I entered, the receptioniste caught my eye. She indicated a man seated in the lobby, obviously waiting to see me. I introduced myself and asked him what he wanted. He immediately accused me of making big profits and suggested that, as a Christian, I was absolutely wrong in having ambition and striving for wealth.

I was more than a little shocked at his outburst, but as it was lunchtime, I invited him into my office to discuss the matter over coffee and sandwiches.

He spent some time telling me how wrong it was to make big profits and build up a business as a Christian. I asked him how much profit he thought I had

made over the last twelve months. His general answer
indicated that he thought I had made quite a bit. I
asked him to be more specific, but he couldn't. I then
proceeded to tell him I had made absolutely no profit
at all over that period, and that if I wasn't careful, I
would go into reverse over the next twelve months.

He was stunned, but I convinced him I was telling
the truth. I then asked him what he did. He admitted
he stayed at home studying while his wife went out
to work. I then questioned him on his wife and children and asked what he considered was his responsibility towards them. Should he not be providing for
and protecting them? A lively discussion followed, but
the outcome of our time together was an apology from
him, and a commitment from him to go out and persevere and grow so that he could give to others. We
shared the Scriptures together and he saw afresh the
great challenge for a Christian to lead and grow and
influence others. He saw the need for leadership.

Wealth leaders *are* needed more now than at any
time in history, and a special breed of biblical benev-
olent wealth leaders is urgently required today to lead
the way and set the course for others to follow. It is
not even sufficient to *say* that others should follow. It
is up to the individual to become so outstanding as to
be recognized by his peers as a leader and others will
follow automatically—just as authority follows respect.
The size of your goal and your eventual achievements
will determine the extent and influence of your wealth
leadership.

A life commitment to Jesus Christ as Lord and
Saviour, together with the acceptance of the totality
of the Holy Scriptures, must come first. This embod-
ies a commitment to all humanity as God's handiwork
and creation, a commitment for the Christian to win
and to help, not through stealth or power, but
through love.

To the impoverished individual, family or nation, financial help with goods and services personally speaks volumes in the language of love. And dare I say, it is impossible to offer help of any kind, under any circumstances, without wealth, because whoever is involved in it must be sustained.

Yes, wealth is leadership and you can be such a leader.

CHAPTER SIX

Wealth Is Power

Wealth can be a good power, if it is earned under the principles of God, developed under the principles of God and used for the principles of God.

CHAPTER SIX

Wealth Is Power

The fact that *wealth is power* would be accepted by almost everyone in the world today. The absence of that power becomes evident whenever you see a need that requires money, and you try to meet that need without money. It always leaves you with a feeling of helplessness.

How often have I heard of a person who is in desperate financial difficulty, and friends and relatives feel absolutely helpless because they do not have the "wealth power" to assist him? Have you ever gone to the bank for an overdraft or a housing loan and had to wait for approval as the banking process unfolds? Frustrating, isn't it? Why don't they just say yes or no? It is the uncertainty that makes you feel so powerless. If only you had the money without all this fuss and bother, you would then have the power over your situation and your financial destiny.

Often we hear of the power of multinationals, and sometimes we wonder if the world system is manipulated by them because of the awesome "wealth power" that they possess. We look at wealthy countries and see the power they yield, and contrast that with other countries which are impotent because they lack this "wealth power".

Occasionally we read of billionaires, and imagine the incredible power they have. Our problem is not in accepting that wealth is power. Our problem is more with understanding how to *handle it* as Christians and recognising the difference between its corruptive and beneficial qualities. One of the difficulties is to discern between what is illusion and what is fact. If I were to ask you how a millionaire lived you would probably fly off into a fantasy, which has little relation to reality, because most people think that a millionaire has the power to do as he chooses. The difference between fantasizing and really living the issue is quite marked; even millionaires actually have little power compared to those who are billionaires! I think the easiest way to explain the situation is to give you an illustration.

The great shipping tycoon Aristotle Onassis was once quietly buying up properties in an area where an oil refinery was to be built. The townspeople were eager to sell their properties because the prices were good. All transactions proceeded without a hitch until it was learnt that an international development was to take place. Upon discovery of the introduction of a "wealth power" organization behind the purchasing of property in their town, the people created a hue and cry against the multinational to get more money. Finally Onassis himself had to go there to settle things down. As he arrived at the terminal building and walked to a waiting car, someone called out from the crowd, "Why are you forcing people out of their homes with money?" The tycoon stopped and replied in a matter of fact way, "You don't force with money . . . you seduce."

And that I believe, in part anyway, is an answer to money's incredible worldly power. Money seduces all kinds of people, including Christians. If you have any doubts about its seductive power, pay particular attention to the next church business meeting you attend and see how many members are seduced into cutting down the stipend when a new pastor is called, so they have greater control. Then contrast that with the standards of seeking, expecting and demanding more for our own daily work. To our shame, it seems commonplace to allow less salaries for Christian full-time workers. The retention of wealth in Christian circles to control and subdue people is power of the worst possible kind.

Recently I was discussing with a company president, his imminent retirement and his need to pass control of his business to a younger man. He informed me that although the younger man would be in charge and bear the title of president, he would, as the owner, shift to a simple but more effective position as "financial controller". He winked and said, "Guess who'll still hold the reins?"

There is no question about the possibility of wealth controlling a person, and some are so obsessed with wealth that the only thing that satisfies them is just a little bit more. Such greed and lust for power can control a person's destiny all the way to hell. It is substantiated in Scripture when it says, "The love of money is the root of all evil" (1 Timothy 6:10). The obsession with it, the power of it, the greed of it, and what you are prepared to do to get it, indicates the hold it has on you.

I think it needs to be said that power is not necessarily leadership. The Christian church has many people in positions of power, but they may never be described as leaders because of their lack of demonstrating leadership qualities. Power holding is *not* leadership and a true leader remains a leader even if the power position or authority is removed. Many wealthy people and companies may have inherited a wealth/power position, but they do not use that power to *lead* others. Quite the contrary, they use it to destroy others with brute force. Lord Acton once said, "Power tends to corrupt; absolute power corrupts absolutely." No Christian will deny that if he had wealth power, he would use it for good. But, I believe that we must accept that there is a corrupting influence in money . . . its power to destroy. Should I then seek further wealth power, and if so, are there any conditions, boundaries or directions which I must work within?

Fire has within it the danger element to destroy. Nevertheless, we all accept the need for fire. In fact, without it civilisation as we know it would grind to a halt. Fire is a double-edged sword—it can hurt as well as help. Money power falls into the same category, and needs to be treated with even more respect.

Wealth *can* be a good power if it's earned under the principles of God, developed under the principles of God, and used for the principles of God. Wealth is not bad, unless you love it more than you love the things of God. In fact, one could argue that because you love the things of God, it ought to encourage you to obtain wealth/power to help perpetuate those same things.

Someone once said to me, "Why do you think money is so important?" I replied, firstly, that Jesus said that where your treasure is, there will your heart be also (Matthew 6:21). That makes it a good indicator of our faith. Secondly, the principle of Luke 6:38 ("Give and it shall be given unto you") is a good developer of our faith. And thirdly, how you get it and what you do when you get it, in a measure determines which direction you are going . . . it helps to develop life principles.

We need wealth to *expand* and *maintain* churches

and ministry programmes. But as soon as we make that statement, someone will always say that we could pray for that increase. My response to that is, "Of course, let's pray but let's also help find an answer to that prayer." We accept that God owns everything, but he has put us on earth as stewards. I have never heard any reports of money falling from heaven in answer to prayer. But I *have* heard of people giving their wealth in response to prayer . . . and that wealth power was provided under God, the power force that gets things done.

If, in fact, people with wealth are needed to respond to prayer, then should it not follow that wealthy Christians should be the primary response to needy Christians' prayer? If that is the case, should not we accept the development of our wealth power, work harder and give it away to help others as well as ourselves? Wealth is power to the Christian church. But it is dormant power, latent power in the hearts and minds of those too lazy to succeed or too timid to confront it full on. We are content to play and flirt with wealth as we use it in our everyday lives, yet we know we could help others if we had more. Could it be Satan has scored again by indicating that involvement at the self-need level is most important?

Wealth is indeed power; power with traps, power to expose weaknesses in ourselves. You see the real reason why it is as difficult for a rich man to enter the kingdom of heaven as it is for a camel to pass through the eye of a needle is that we are not prepared to separate wealth from ourselves, and become trusting servants on behalf of our Master. God is all powerful, and if we accept that wealth is power under trusteeship, then our churches and Christian programmes need not be impoverished or dormant. They can explode. Wealth used to glorify God is indeed of great power.

CHAPTER SEVEN

Wealth Is Influence

It became obvious to the person on the phone he was now faced with an equal opponent with a proven track record and resources available. The case was dropped. Wealth is influence ...

CHAPTER SEVEN

Wealth Is Influence

I was going broke for the second time. A meeting had been called for me to meet all my creditors, most of them angry.

My accountants stood with me at the front of the room and everything looked black. It seemed as though they would close me down and wipe me out without a chance in the world of being able to make good.

Suddenly, one person, who was a respected man with large business interests, stood up and said: "I believe that Mr. Daniels can turn the situation around if we give him an opportunity to go back into business . . ." It was at that point I was given the chance to try and prove myself once again. That man, because of his wealth and position, had *influence* and was able to sway the creditors to the point where I was given a second shot to prove to one and all that I had the stickability to hang in and win. Never let it be said that wealth does not have influence.

Many people display their character by declaring they treat all people alike; those with special economic advantage—however large—are treated the same as anyone else. I am not suggesting as a Christian that it should be any other way.

But in reality one would have to be blind not to notice that the world gives attention to those who, largely because of financial position, ability or leadership, are respected for their achievements and receive special attention. This attention can be simply a matter of seat placement at a dinner or public meeting. Or it could be an enquiry from the mass media for an opinion. In every society, there is usually in every street the best and worst house. And on that basis alone the occupants, without any other pressure generally, allocate a difference between the two lifestyles in regard to influence.

Wealth has the same effect, whether it be in primitive native tribes or large affluent cities, it means influence.

If an individual, through hard work and good planning, creates a position of wealth for himself, then others who come into contact with him will usually accept his position of influence. Wealth as influence can arise out of a simple *respect* for a person's achievement in society. And he is usually the sort of person who can "pull strings". He is able to deal with problems, seemingly insurmountable to many, by a simple phone call. This brings me to what I call "third person influence."

First, let us recognise that everyone of us has some wealth influence, irrespective of our financial place within society. It means simply discerning where you stand and how you are evaluated by others—how much better off you are, to put it bluntly. Now, on that basis alone, you should realise you can help others with your influence. Indeed, if you are a Christian, dare I say you *must*. This is where "third person influence" comes into play.

A case in point occurred when I was once

approached by an immigrant who needed help from a government minister. Because he presented himself so badly through his aggressive nature, he was never given an appointment. This man was brought to me and in some way I was able to unravel the story, make a phone call and gain an audience for the unfortunate immigrant. An obvious third party influence comes in when you phone a company on behalf of someone else looking for a job.

Before I look at the *boundaries* on using wealth as an influence, I will take one more case history as an example. An individual was once introduced to me who, it was blatantly obvious, had been taken advantage of in a contract. Legal pressures were building up and so were the expenses. I examined the case and then during the course of the day I rang the person who I considered was unfairly oppressing this man. I simply said I was prepared to enter the arena and help. It became obvious to the person on the phone he was now faced with an equal opponent with a proven track record and resources available. The case was dropped. Wealth was influence. But, like other areas of life, this influence has its boundaries, ground rules of propriety, as I would call them.

It is improper to *demand* that someone's influence be used and so make your problems a burden to someone else. Neither should you ever make commitments on behalf of someone else. "I know someone who will be able to fix this up, so let's go ahead and do it. If it goes wrong, we'll give him a call . . ." You get the picture. On the other hand, we should put ourselves out if the need is there, and it requires a compassionate use of wealth influence. A doctor friend of mine told me of his daughter and son-in-law living interstate who needed a home badly. They had apparently saved a reasonable amount of money, but housing prices were high and, although they had made enquiries, a mortgage seemed unattainable. It was a very simple matter for me to talk to my bank manager and get him to make a call to his branch office interstate. The bank managers discussed the situation and decided it would be a good thing to help out as I was a respected client. The mortgage went through.

However, I am appalled at the number of commitments people have made on my behalf over the past years with absolutely no respect for my time or interest. They have felt that merely on the basis that they met me on one occasion, they were entitled to make any number of commitments on my behalf. Many of these things I find I'm ill-equipped to deal with, or simply do not want to become involved in.

The other side of wealth and influence is the danger of using your influence *too much* for the same people. There is the hazard that you will eventually be let down and find yourself obligated to the person you are seeking to influence. Also, bear in mind you have an "influence quota"—using your influence on minor or trifling matters will use up that quota and when the big need arises your influence may be spent. Be prepared to say *no*.

I think it is vital to continue to expand your sphere of influence, and to this end I keep a file index on people in areas of importance. Your influence is something that must be used, because it is part of who you are and what you stand for, and as a result, demonstrates the depth of your character. It is important to recognise influence and use it. And we all have it. By law we have the influence of casting a vote; by constitutional freedom we can write to the press and speak on talk-back radio. You also have influence within the family circle; that is unchallengeable. The question is, do you have the courage, tact and discipline to use it correctly?

The individual who has wealth, at whatever measure, is especially obligated to use his influence. To withhold such dynamic power, or restrict and deny its full potential, is very grave indeed. For those with wealth who have a heart to help others, it will not take long to find that wealth is influence.

CHAPTER EIGHT

Wealth Is Pressure

The pressure to avoid pressure is so pressurised that many feel pressurised not to accept the pressure and place themselves under pressure trying to avoid that pressure . . .

CHAPTER EIGHT

Wealth Is Pressure

There is no doubt we are living in the fast lane. The keyword today is *pressure*. We are in a world of speed, economic change, the micro-chip and fast shifts in power bases. Just coping with the opportunities and difficulties at home, at our place of employment and in church life places us under pressure. There are those who would escape pressure by adopting a counter culture—dropping out and removing themselves from society and its very presence. But they still keep their options open in regard to health care and social assistance when required. Quite often this lifestyle represents an escape from pressure by simply ignoring a responsibility to the rest of the population, including the payment of taxes and involvement in assistance programmes.

As I speak to people in churches, homes and in the business and government spheres, I hear a tidal wave of complaints about those day-to-day pressures of life. It is time we were reminded that pressure is *nothing new*. I doubt whether the pressure today is any less intense than that of a century ago, and I doubt the pressure of family life is very much different—

although I concede there is a difference in style.

An investigation into life a century ago (by thumbing through books at the public library) will make you keenly aware of the pressures faced by those of yesteryear. There were the ravages of disease, overworked children, the lack of welfare help, virtual slave labor and women living in almost total bondage. There was also virtually no regulation in regard to food and hygiene. There was war, hazards of world travel and little protection against the elements. Why, even life expectancy was shortened through the sheer pressures of living . . . The difference is that today we have more experts to discuss, dissect and probe the problems of pressure, in turn increasing our awareness of the problems that surround us. Pressure is bad when you accept it in the negative, making it a frustrating part of your life. But it can be good when looked at in a positive way, an indicator to the areas in your life where you can improve and grow.

The pressure to avoid pressure is so pressurised that many feel pressurised not to accept the pressure and place themselves under pressure trying to avoid that pressure! But never forget this: avoidance of pressure is the avoidance of the *realities* of life and, indeed, life itself. That is because the very existence of day-to-day living is based on accepting pressure and turning it into a challenge; quite simply, it means we face pressure to meet life's daily needs.

I have known of some Christians who were under so much pressure to escape pressure that they fled to the country to retire from life. It was then they found they suffered internal guilt pressures, as well as finding a whole new set of different problems—and more pressure! Some feel pressured to do and others feel pressured not to do. And we should remember a great deal of pressure is based in our *imagination*. That pressure which is real on the other hand, can represent a threat to the status quo, or it may represent an opportunity and even a challenge for growth. It is up to the Christian to demonstrate that a relationship with God, who is sovereign, gives him a formula for turning pressure into treasure. And through that process he will learn more about himself in respect to the acceptance to Scriptural calls upon his life.

I recall reading a one and a half page letter from a friend in Brisbane, Queensland, named Lindsay. All through the letter, Lindsay was telling me about the pressure he was experiencing through criticism, innuendo, outright lies and accusations by those who were formerly his friends. He was trying to build a business so that he could give and he was starting to succeed. But through the success, he found the envy and misunderstanding of others being thrust upon him. As I read through the long lament I started to laugh and the further I got, the more I laughed, until the tears were almost rolling down my cheeks. I picked up the phone to comfort my friend and when he answered he asked, "Have you got my letter? I'm sorry it's so full of problems. I hope it didn't discourage you."

I replied, "As soon as I started reading through it, I laughed and couldn't stop laughing."

"Why were you laughing when I was hurting?" he demanded.

I explained, "I was laughing because you are now starting to walk down the corridor of wealth and are finding out, as others have before you, that wealth is pressure." I welcomed him into his new-found arena and encouraged him to continue to higher ground, ignoring the comments from the crowd. Lindsay started to understand then, as he does more than ever now, that wealth is pressure.

Biblical figures were under extreme pressure. Some pressures were caused by people, others by timing and events. Look at Moses and the children of Israel. Or,

David and Solomon. Or, Paul. He endured a lifestyle
and schedule of work and commitment which would
devastate many of the high-powered executives of
today. Then, of course, there was Jesus Christ, continually under a state of pressure as he went about His
ministry.

Some may find it hard to believe that *wealth is pressure*. It is a rarely-talked-about pressure. Incredible
pressure. Continuing pressure. Urgent pressure. And,
at times, wealth is pressure just by its very existence.
That is often compounded by scriptural instruction
such as good stewardship and providing for the needs
of others. Wealth also creates more pressure because
it is more exposed and vulnerable, and the biblical
requirement stating, "To whom much is given, from
him much will be required" (Luke 12:48) is more
demanding. One of the great pressures of wealth is
the need to learn to continually adapt to change.
There are such considerations as changes within the
market place, variations within our own economies,
the aspect of inflation, changes in personnel, altered
travel schedules, time zones and international
exchange.

A worker who is committed to stay in the same job
for twenty years may be affected by some changes,
but the pressure on him is not as diversified or as
relentless as one who is dealing with wealth.

And pressure can be very personal. Quite often I
will find myself on an international telephone call with
two or more calls banked up. There is a double telex
to be answered and a sales contract on my desk waiting to be ratified. A person has dropped in to see
me—without an appointment. I am under pressure.
What do I do? There are some who will say, "Let go
and let God." But I did let go and let God take over
my life twenty years ago. And I prayed, and always
will pray, that he will give me the wisdom and energy

to handle whatever He chooses to bring across my path today. Others may suggest that I delegate more. Others may recommend, "Do what you can do comfortably and leave the rest." But I must reply that I am under the conviction of Luke 6:38. When God gave me wealth, he gave with it a responsibility, and now I must accept the pressure of the acquisition and its distribution.

It also has been suggested to me many times that I should share my pressures with someone else. As I contemplate that, I respond with the question: Should I share my pressure problems with my competitor? He would at least be one who would appreciate the complexities. I am sure he would be interested to know that I have particular problems. But I am arrested by the thought that if I tell him, it could be an unwise move because I would have the additional pressure of competing against him from a disadvataged position.

Should I share my pressure problems, doubts and anxieties with my bank manager, to obtain some sort of mental relief? If I do, I will soon find out the bank wants to know what I am going to do in resolving the problems which are causing the pressures. I will lose their confidence and be placed under more pressure!

Some well meaning person once suggested that I share my pressures with my staff. But I pulled up sharply at that idea because my staff need me to relieve *their* pressures and doubts. In a Catch-22 situation, their pressure will be increased by an eroding of their confidence in me. I am naturally the one they look to for leadership. In a sense I will have doubled my trouble.

Often the advice is given to share my pressures with my wife, so she can help carry the burden. But if I understand my Bible correctly, I should protect her and not burden her. And if I did tell her, then maybe *she* may be pressured to worry about me being under so much pressure. Once again, I will have additional pressure as a result of her worry, and double my trouble.

Sharing with a friend is not going to be much easier; pressure is very much like pain—it cannot be shared. And very often in the effort to share and dwell upon the magnitude and discomfort of pressure, it is increased by the act of regurgitation.

Generally speaking, if God has given you a vision of involvement and achievement, do not expect anyone to fully appreciate the pressure levels of that vision, because it is a personal vision for you alone, and it is rare for another person to relate on that personal wave length.

At the close of an address I gave one evening on goal setting to the management of staff of a large manufacturing company, a young man in his 30's approached me and said, "Because of the talk you have just given, I am going to set a goal to take my wife and children for a holiday in about two years time." I commended him on his newly found goal and I asked the young man why he was going to leave it until two years to have a holiday. Then he told me how much pressure he would be inflicting on himself to do it earlier. If there was any way possible of doing it earlier, he would, but it was just too much pressure.

I then asked the young man, "Do you love your family?" He replied that he loved them dearly. I invited him to see in his mind's eye his wife and children before a firing squad and to imagine their lives would be forfeited if he was unable to take them away for a holiday within the next twelve months. I then asked him the question again. "Is it possible for you to take your family away within twelve months under that type of pressure?" He replied smartly, "I'll take them away within the next six months!"

It is almost unbelievable the games we play in our minds, even at the expense of those we love, to avoid pressure.

After a lecture programme on commitment at Bible College, at question time a young lady asked the question, "Ought not we to share our faults with one another?" I asked her if she would mind sharing a fault with us. She commented on her continued difficulty in getting up early in the morning. No sooner did the words leave her mouth than a young man at the back of the class called out, "I have the same problem!" I then enquired of the young lady, "Do you feel better, knowing that others have experienced the same pressure difficulties?" She said it was a great relief and of great help to know that others had the same difficulty.

My next question was a very simple one, and that was, "Now that you know someone else has the same problem, hasn't that knowledge taken the edge off of your challenge to correct it?" She admitted quite sheepishly that it had. This is an important lesson. We sometimes try to avoid pressure by diluting it. Finding someone else who shares the guilt we carry, we placate ourselves and ignore the problem.

We need to accept the fact that life is pressure. While we continue to live on this earth there will be pressures. And if you accept the responsibility of acquiring and distributing wealth around the nation, then you will carry the pressure of commitment.

It is true that possessions create pressure even under trusteeship. The trustee will find—and must accept—the pressure of acquiring, managing and developing the sharing of wealth from his position.

To give means very often to become involved in planning, policy making and decision making at many different levels and under many different flags. And the pressure is always there to do it well, decently and in order with compassion and understanding. Pressure can be a real *growth* experience. If you accept the pressure of a commitment, with the right measurement of time and effectiveness, that pressure will thrust you to unknown heights of experience and Christian growth.

By this time, you are probably asking the question: "Is there no relief or escape from pressure—if only temporarily?" The answer is a definite "yes".

There are several methods I have employed to take the edge off pressure, or at least to arm me in preparation for it.

One is a solid routine, which incorporates fitness of the body with soundness of mind. I start my day with a run. Rain or shine I make this a daily ritual. I have promised myself I will run each weekday until my seventieth birthday. I feel better for it; it clears my head and gives me the chance to think about what lies ahead for the day. Once back in the house, I make my wife a cup of tea and take it to her with a fresh flower. (This some men find intimidating. I mentioned it once in an address and one woman leaned over to her husband and gave him a nudge saying: "Are you tuning in?" "Oh yes," said he, "but his wife's probably worth it!")

I then read the Scriptures aloud with my wife and then we pray. This daily routine is a trade secret. But try it—it works. Once I am involved in the day-to-day running of my business the pressure may start to mount. If I find it is getting too great, I will sometimes whip out my personal affirmation book and take a quick tally of my past achievements. I have kept this book for many years, and after a quick read through it, I come out a shouting optimist.

Also take note here that during times of intense pressure you should check your reading habits. I make sure that I am not studying military history at the

time, but rather biographies of people who have over-
come difficulties.

A sauna and a spa followed by a massage can also
work wonders when the going is tough.

Once a week, usually Thursday for me—I make my
way down to the public library and find a quiet corner
where I can sit and think. Not read, just think, med-
itate, review and rehabilitate myself. Marvellous
therapy!

I have always maintained private prayer, Scripture
reading and meditating upon the Word of God is *the*
rejuvenating encouragement one needs. It leads to
balance and is a powerful motivating factor. To continually avoid pressure is to dismiss the interaction and
challenge of life, and demonstrates an unwillingness
to become involved in the race of life. I repeat again
the scriptural injunction: "To whom much is given,
from him much will be required." Wealth is pressure.

Wealth Is Sacrifice

What I am saying is that you cannot go through life playing games and putting off the inevitable—if you do not give, you do not get.

CHAPTER NINE

Wealth Is Sacrifice

The phrase "there is no such thing as a free lunch" is mouthed by many but believed by few. While it is true, on occasion, that we do get something for nothing due to circumstance or benevolence, universal law dictates you must put out to pull in. If this were not the case, then the world would not progress, people would not develop, crops would not be planted, students would never learn and no one would achieve. It is the wrestling against the percentages of the unknown that produces character. Not knowing how much more training one has to do to win an Olympic Gold and not knowing how much you have to give in services to become wealthy are the unknown factors. What this means in substance is if you want something out of life, then you must put something in. And I have found that generally the more planned proportion you put in, the more guaranteed return you will get out, irrespective of your chosen field.

I put emphasis on *planned output*. So often people talk to me about their enormous output into life and complain about the return—once again we see misspent energy. In not *planning* your output there is the ever-present danger of becoming a slave to circumstances and even accepting an existence of robotisation.

Moses accepted a life plan. Joseph accepted a life plan. David and Paul accepted a life plan. So too did John the Baptist. And Jesus humbled himself in the form of man to accept a life plan.

As one reads the journals of history (I have read more than 1100 biographies), it becomes plain to see that planning combined with output and timing are keys to any wealth quotient. These things require *sacrifice*. Wealth in any field requires sacrifice. But even in the centre of sacrifice there is a quiet happiness because one learns to understand deep down that the giving of oneself to a worthy cause or event brings with it satisfaction. However, it is important to define clearly what you are prepared to sacrifice to reach your wealth quotient.

I recall once sitting with some of the largest corporate executives in America. We were discussing the recession in the late seventies. One turned to the other and asked how he thought he would cope with the down turn. The answer was, "I'm not prepared to join it." He went on to explain he was going to make some sacrifices. They would be planned sacrifices, organised and timed to deal with the current climate. He would trim his ship, he would cut where necessary, he would develop new skills, sharpen his wits and discipline his life. He knew that he had to sacrifice certain aspects of his business and his life to stay in the market and thrive.

Results over the past few years have shown that his wealth sacrifice proved to be right. He is now among the top business leaders in the United States, and going on to bigger and better things.

Sacrifice will mean different things to different people. To some, it may mean time away from family and friends or restrictions on time and leisure. To others, it may mean a cluttered mind and stress along with the sacrifice of sleep. It could also mean the postponement of holidays and an increase in risk-taking. To many, sacrifice will mean added tension, personal pressure and the sacrifice of past security factors like a steady wage, superannuation and job security. Consider here that risk-taking is not only a necessary part of life, but planned risk is closely associated with the wealth quotient factor—people who risk the most gain the most.

I remember all too clearly those who challenged me years ago about my harsh discipline on my life and the results of such a lifestyle on my family. It meant that at times I was unable to be with them because of travel, study or just plain exhaustion. But for the record, let it be noted, when I *was* with them, we savoured every moment and used every occasion to build relationships, to assess disciplines and just have fun.

And I would say to my critics that later, as our children were about to move into the teenage years, we were able to buy a farm and spend weekends together. These were times of fishing, hunting and long walks or just sitting around a log fire, talking. We spent those days together, exchanging our love and thoughts as a result of earlier sacrifice. And the bottom line to all this was that because we had that time together we did not experience problems with our children later.

I am not suggesting *what* one should sacrifice; that, I believe, is a matter of personal choice. What I am saying is that you cannot go through life playing games and putting off the inevitable—if you do not give, you do not get. And I maintain it is wise to sacrifice some time in earlier years to prepare for a more comfortable and satisfying life in later years. I read somewhere, and I am sure it is true, that nothing binds like poverty and old age.

Sacrifice is also a *relative* issue. In a wealthy country the sacrifices you feel are not so great when you consider the world scene as a whole. Many endure suffering and sacrifice, not of their own choosing, but because of dictatorship or corrupt regimes. Consider your sacrifice compared to that of a refugee sacrificing everything for freedom.

Those with wealth should consider the sacrifice of their time and money by taking the lead and encouraging others to become involved in planned action. I maintain that the continuous sacrifice of the wealthy, who are sensitive to the needs of others, is a lifelong involvement. Take a case in point—planned giving to a Bible College or missionary society.

But that is only part of the involvement I mentioned; the other is *personal involvement*. While you may satisfy a financial need, it may also be necessary for you to give of your management expertise and time in the long run. Boring directors' meetings are often more sacrificial than giving that money! But it is an obligation, and I believe it goes with the whole package.

Sometimes you may be called upon to help an individual with a business or personal problem. The easy way out would be to offer dollars and cents; get them to go away and leave you alone. But you must continue the sacrifice with personal involvement, because the return on past sacrifices you have made has put you in a position to help. Wealth is not an idealistic life of beach-combing.

It is an individual, deep involvement and a continuing relationship with the human race. Wealth is sacrifice. And it is not a sacrifice without its critics. Have you ever faced the criticism of "conscience saving" or "buying popularity?" It is often the case that the higher the wealth quotient, the greater the accusations, even when you give sacrificially. Wealth gives public prominence, which in turn frequently attracts group criticism, judgement and lack of privacy. Wealth also brings a continual flow of requests from businesses and organisations you do not know or even have any sympathy with.

The most exciting thing about wealth sacrifice is that it can bring great pleasure, satisfaction and joy if you continually give of yourself and your quotient. Others may see you in the light of their own circumstance and framework. But you have the quiet edge on them in your own conscience and can certainly live happily with yourself if you learn that wealth sacrifice can be a positive force for good. But you must keep the rules.

1. Accept that your God-given wealth is a tool.
2. Accept that you must sacrifice the substance of that tool in order to increase its strength and to make it useful.
3. Accept that you are going to make mistakes and give unwisely at times and use that to strengthen the rule to give, not to hold back.
4. Accept that your personality is directly associated with your wealth sacrifice and very often they must be given together.
5. Accept a new big challenge every few years to stop the rot from setting in.
6. Remember that you are in good company. The greatest sacrifice the world has ever known was made 2,000 years ago and mankind has been benefiting because of it ever since and will be forever.

How do you become happy, though rich? Sacrifice your wealth, your time, your personality; but remember that you do not have the right or authority to sacrifice others.

CHAPTER TEN

Wealth Means Criticism

In my lifetime I have seen more destruction and more crushing of the human spirit through this medium than through any other type of dehumanising abuse . . .

CHAPTER TEN

Wealth
Means Criticism

For the person of wealth—anyone who has more than someone else—there are three things of which you can be certain:
1. You are going to die sometime.
2. You are going to pay taxes.
3. You are going to be criticised.

Believe me, *criticism* is as certain as the other two, and yet most people think once they have a few dollars their troubles will fall away. The fact of the matter is quite simple. It is this: a few more dollars may solve some problems, but the more wealth you have, the greater the criticism you receive—and it is directly proportional to the amount of wealth or standing you are perceived of having.

I think the youth of today are probably guilty, if not more guilty than the older generation, in their selective type of wealth criticism. It seems quite okay for the punk rocker, the rock superstar or the film star to be bedecked in all types of jewellery, to drive limousines or to live in mansions. But as soon as a youngster's boss or neighbour exhibits any such riches he is targeted. He is criticised for being a "rip-off merchant" and becomes a victim of the "what about" syndrome. We hear the cry of "What about the poor?" and—more specifically—"What about me, then?" Criticism is not restricted to the non-believer. Even Christians and the Christian church launch the occasional attack against wealth, often from a Biblical background of well-selected quotes. This is frequently done with an ignorance of the true wealth the church may have in its real estate holdings!

Much criticism is shallow, but can have an effect. I learned this lesson when I found myself chairman of a large city crusade. Numbers were down on some nights and the collections were getting frighteningly low in respect to the budget we had to meet. So I would go out on the platform in the evening and challenge people to give. Out of the thousands of people present, we received three notes in the collection plate requesting I stop asking for money. Some of my fellow board members came to me with the notes and I allowed the criticism to get to me. I was told to wait and the money would come in. I tried that for two nights and the results were more alarming. I went back to giving the challenge and encouraging the assemblage to give as a spiritual commitment. The funds came in as a result of the strength of the challenge.

It was interesting to note that those who came to me with the request to water down the challenge disappeared at the end of the crusade, and there was still a deficit to be met. I was the one left alone to meet the deficit. I never saw or heard from my accusers again.

I learnt that even the mention of money brings criticism. And at that time I carried the full burden of the effect of that criticism.

Having *accepted* that criticism is going to occur, and that it will be continual, let us look at it more deeply and attempt to gain an insight and some solutions.

The first thing we need to understand is the nature of the *critic*, who as judge, jury and executioner, often presupposes that he has the criteria for criticism. He *assumes* that he has all the facts; the absolute ability to form an expert judgement on those facts; the judicial ability to form an expert judgement; the authority to make critical comments and enforce the sentence.

Now, while we can accept that anyone with a wealth quotient has their life up for scrutiny, I think all of us would agree there would be few—if any—critics that would qualify under the above framework. I suppose, when we are talking about the really honest critic, then we have to make allowances. But even with the honest critic, he or she has an obligation to become part of the solution by showing us how to solve the problem!

The unfortunate thing about criticism, which is rarely exposed, is that it is usually *loveless*, because by its very action it pulls down the victim and elevates the accuser. *It is the great tool of the unmotivated.*

In my travels and involvement in the business world, I have generally found that the biggest critics do the least work. They may point out the problem, and sometimes the solution, but they rarely follow through with action. Many is the time you will challenge people about their criticism and they will tritely answer that they were only *commenting* on what should or could be done. We should therefore understand the difference between the comment and the criticism. Simply put, a comment is non-judgemental, non-destructive and non-personal; criticism is invariably a proxy for involvement.

If it seems I have come down harshly on the critic, it is because in my lifetime I have seen more destruction and more crushing of the human spirit through this medium than any other type of dehumanising abuse. Too often, critics presuppose that they know better and that they can do better without the involvement. It is very much a backhanded boasting without having to put up one's own life for scrutiny. I think it is one of the worst forms of deceit.

At this point I would like to mention group criticism. I regard group criticism as a reinforced ego-expander which puffs up the critics and gives them an artificial feeling of power. They attack a group of people—or, as they perceive it—a group of leaders. But it should be recognised that a leaders' meeting does not mean we have a group of leaders meeting! Leaders break new ground, possess wealth, fame and prominence. Still, such a gathering is fair game to the critic who will stand back and attack from afar. Bear in mind, the critic usually cannot handle personal criticism himself. He often adopts aloofness of spirit as a guard against criticism himself. The ways to handle criticism are:

1. Accept that the critic has ego needs that may only be satisfied by continuing criticism.
2. Accept that you have an opportunity to declare the facts and deter further criticism.
3. Do not belittle a critic, as you will only put yourself in his league and be just as guilty of dehumanisation.
4. Try and ignore criticism altogether; you are unlikely to miss anything of value.

Wealth Is Courage

But now, more than ever before, God needs faithful stewards who have the courage to move forward and upwards in their economic life . . .

CHAPTER ELEVEN

Wealth Is Courage

I had my back to the wall . . . I was going down for the third time. Once again my creditors were closing in, but I still knew I could make it. But that was not easy stuck in the middle of the Nullarbor Plain with a broken axle!

In a bid to fight back financially, I had resolved to journey to Perth in Western Australia. I was doing it on a minimum budget and was becoming increasingly aware of the problems facing me as I struck one pothole in the road after another. Every so often, a kangaroo would spring out across the road and sometimes a wild brumby would appear in the headlight beam. The inevitable happened—I hit a bad pothole and the axle collapsed.

There I was a thousand miles from anywhere with little hope of sighting another vehicle until at least the next day. I had one can of peaches to eat, and the night air was freezing. That night, I heated the peaches on a fire and felt the desperation creeping in. I had a business to run but nowhere to go and nothing to take me there. At times like that, we need courage.

Wealth means courage and getting wealth requires

courage. Wealth means courage when you are faced
with economic downturn, when you have to stand out
in a crowd or when you are told you will not make
it and you resolve to pursue and win.

I resolved to win out in the Nullarbor. I knew you
only fail when you stop trying. I went on to be
successful after that trip. But I failed again! By any
benchmark, courage requires we be *different*. A great
philosopher once spoke about the cowardliness of
conformity. Most people draw their lives from the
direction of others. In Western Society it is easier to
follow the crowd, and it is relatively easy to make a
living.

But now, more than ever before, God needs faithful
stewards who have the courage to move forward and
upwards in their economic life, to become bastions of
support by their courageous deeds in those economic
halls of power. This applies to all walks of life. Because
a farmer keeps planting after devastating droughts, by
his courageous commitment to succeed, we in turn
have a loaf of bread on our table. Very often we have
to endure the humility of failure to understand exactly
what measure of courage is required to start again;
what measure of optimism and God-inspired
confidence we need to win through.

I think we also need to be reminded at this point
that it is not arrogance, folly or pride that challenges
the Bible-believing Christian to wealth. It is *courage*.
The kind of courage that inspired our great explorers
and missionaries to venture into the unknown. That
same courage is needed today for the Christian who
must step into the wilderness of economic change. We
are in a time of revolution on all fronts and the courage of commitment is needed.

That courage was rediscovered many years ago by
men like R. G. LeTourneau and Charles Mott who
showed that the Christian order of economics had the

answer for the likes of Karl Marx.

Wealth courage is not for the timid steward; it is totally different from the achievements in any other field. If you spend courageous years on academic attainment, you will retain that knowledge. If you persevere and exercise courage in the area of music, your fruits will be enjoyed long after you have departed this earth. Sporting achievements also require courage and determination, evidenced by the reaching of goals that can be recorded and witnessed.

But wealth courage is different. It is fleeting and fanciful. It leaves no great records and if you have one failure you can lose it all, and possibly be under suspicion for life.

To create wealth from scratch you may have to work until your bones ache and your brain feels it may burst. You are often called on to inspire those around you as you forge ahead. It takes a special kind of courage to handle the pressures, speed and criticism associated with the reach for wealth.

This reminds me of the time I was having great difficulties making ends meet, selling from town to town, but without funds to buy a decent meal. I carried a little spirit burner and a quantity of cooking fat. Every so often I would buy a small quantity of potatoes and cook them in my cramped hotel room over that little burner. I used to wave the fumes out of the window with my hat in case the proprietor found out what I was doing. This was one of the desperate measures I resorted to to build a business. It also took more than a little courage.

Then again, there can be such a thing as *misplaced courage*; a confusion over direction resulting in energy mis-spent. Recently on television I saw a team of people demonstrating for more money to be spent on children's rights. The team in question was walking around Australia to collect funds for their cause. A courageous feat, without question. The planning and back-up teams were substantial and the man-hours required to mount the quest must have been colossal. After three thousand kilometres one of the organisers said he was disappointed with the response—they had raised a mere $240.

That team no doubt had courage—the courage to face hardship for a cause. But I question the method, the thought process behind the event. I did some simple arithmetic. The demonstration took about twelve weeks. Multiply that by fifty people, then combine that with a modest salary of, say, $200 per week. That brings us to a total expenditure of $120,000! (not including back-up costs). By any criteria the raising of $240 in this case was an example of wasted energy— and courage.

I feel a more practical way to help the physically or mentally handicapped is by the individual approach. Why not go into a business and give those less fortunate the chance to work? It will do more for their self esteem than any amount of counselling and walks around the country. And on the individual's part it will mean a Christian approach to making wealth and spreading it around.

Even in the churches, we spend enormous time and effort on fund raising fetes and promotions requiring high energy input to raise small sums of money. It is a pursuit that would not reach the table of consideration in the business field. What is needed is a revolution and courageous commitment in our attitudes towards wealth. Have you noticed how the fire of enthusiasm for a project collapses when it is suggested we give a day's wage to the cause?

The *first step* in the revolution of values is a measure of commitment, because so often *we* are not committed, although we want *others* to be. Remember, when all is said and done, more is usually said than done.

The *second step* is the awakening to the fact that wealth is power. It is a fact nations accept and industry accepts. We may acknowledge it in the day-to-day purchasing power we have, but not as a means of fighting the cause for others.

The *third step* is having the courage to put what we believe into *action*; the real courage required to become involved at an economic and personal level.

It does not take real courage to go with the crowd in a group action, but it does require courage to go it alone and create jobs and upgrade people's attitudes and aspirations.

It takes courage to treat fellow humans with fairness and integrity and win in the economic race to bless others with a Christian commitment.

Wealth is courage when you follow the New Testament example of being light in a darkened world. It is the Christian who will, with faith, lead the way economically and substantiate a revolution of values, by the commitment of his wealth. If you go broke in the process, a new kind of courage that has been tried and tested will make you get up and try again.

Many times I have seen big men, not only physically, but spiritually, crack under the weight of economic and business downturn. At that point the courageous ones bounce back with renewed vigour and tempered attitudes. The church today will be further impoverished if Christians do not accept the challenge of exercising courage in the attainment of wealth for the benefit of all.

CHAPTER TWELVE

Wealth Is For You

Wealth is for you, but one of the down payments is a preparation to accept total personal responsibility . . .

CHAPTER TWELVE

Wealth Is
For You

Wealth is for you if you *want* it. It is as profound
as it is simple. Your faith commitment will tell the
story as to exactly what value you put on your journey
through life. Commitment and evidence of that
commitment glorifies God. Excusers blame God. I
have always considered that if we ignore the
abundances of the universe and human potential we
actually minimise God's creative hand, and in turn,
limit our own life's power.

It is plain for all to see the earth and human life is
more than abundant. There are more animals, sun,
air and water than we can use. And there are more
ideas, intellect, motivation and wisdom locked within
ourselves, simply waiting for release through faith.

We need to "stir up the gift that is within us," and
by doing so, light the fuse that will explode and let
the riches flow for the benefit of all. But courageous
Christians must lead the way.

Wealth is there for us to grasp (within Christian
principles) and to distribute under Christian grace;
and most of the world is waiting for that selfless act.
They are waiting to recognise the fact that Christian

men and women will do what no one else will do: give, keep on giving and keep on earning to give more.

We should realise that we possess incalculable wealth. If not in money, then in ideas, labor, care, counsel, knowledge and, of course, love. The way to expand it—to ensure its retention—is to give it away. But beware that you do not concentrate on one area; the area that is the simplest one, or the one that feels good. We should seek to become well-rounded persons in our giving and we will become well-rounded personalities in return. We so often hear of the wealthy person who gives money to appease his conscience, knowing full well that true giving means total giving, without boundaries.

If you diligently plan for it and eagerly work at it, wealth can be for you. But the pursuit of wealth must always be within the bounds of biblical principles and personal responsibility.

The first step is to recognise the abundance of God's goodness which is close at hand, then step outside of yourself and recognise the needs of others.

Bear in mind at this point that the only human being God has given you total control over—under His grace—is *you*. Therefore, you must start right where you are with an attitude of mind and spirit that you not only have a responsibility, but that you possess the necessary equipment to fulfil that responsibility. No longer can you accept that the obligation to build that church, fund that mission programme or undertake that crusade belongs to others. It is now a personal responsibility, for you are personally accountable. No longer should you allow the government to educate your children or the system to sweep you along. Remember, you who are created in the image of God are equal to any challenge the world may throw your way.

Wealth is for you, but it may mean wrestling with the

problem of mathematics in the business economy. *Wealth is for you* if you are prepared to build a better product, give a better service, create a better idea, and persistently with genuine concern be a "people person" of better character. In other words you should have the desire to create wealth for a noble purpose and believe that you can. You must be *convinced*.

I believe the most neglected area of wealth involvement is in the field of consistent, expanded and deep-activated *thought*. Everything starts with a thought or an idea, and you can develop the smallest and most insignificant idea into a Mount Everest of concept. It could even have world-wide implications that may mean personal involvement for you at a level which may elevate your total thinking process to a desperate plateau.

Many times it is easy to be convinced, but to carry out that conviction and pay the price of involvement, cuts across what I call our "human protection barrier". We do not want to be put up for public scrutiny. *Wealth is for you*, but one of the down payments is a preparation to accept total personal responsibility. *Wealth also is for you* if you are prepared to handle it. To earn wealth is one thing, but to be responsible and to manage it, is quite another. Believe it or not, most people earn a fortune from the day they take a job to the day they stop. What makes an individual stand apart is the decision he makes to expand his boundaries and increase his efforts to obtain wealth. Rare are those who earn it, manage to expand it, preserve it, and give it away.

I once met a wealthy man who was totally in control of his wealth—because God was in control of him. He was a Chinese businessman who, I learnt, had an incredible track record of spiritual commitment and giving. He had a far larger business than I, with more influence and more ability. I found myself chatting to him in a hotel lobby, and the conversation came around to giving. He looked me squarely in the eye and asked if I tithed. I said, "Yes."

He asked if I was aware there was in Scripture provision to double tithe, and he asked me if I did it. I said "Yes" again.

He then asked me, "Do you accept the scriptural call for offerings?" to which I replied I did. A smile came on his face, and he enquired if I understood that the further step was gifts. I said I did and that I gave.

"Have you ever considered taking God on as a partner in your business", he asked suddenly. I had to admit at that point, although I had thought about it, I could not come to grips with the reality of it.

A sour lemon look came over his face, and I waited for his response. He stated quite clearly that to have God as a partner in my business would indicate equality, and we could never be on an equal footing with God.

I asked him. "How do you run your business?" His face lit up like a thousand neon lights.

"God has fifty-one per cent of the share and I have forty-nine per cent," he answered. "He has total control!"

Here was a man who gave, who knew the scriptural base for giving, and who knew that placing his wealth—and his life—in God's hands was the only Christian way to handle wealth. He was a rarity.

I consider money as just a tool to be stored properly, allocated in different ways, and retained to allow for opportunities. And like a tool, it is kept sharp for big jobs.

Always keep cash reserves, a working amount, and keep money growing. Always keep cash expanding and keep a giving programme, also expanding. *Wealth is for you* to protect and give.

CHAPTER THIRTEEN

Wealth, The Challenge

It is obvious to me that what is lacking in our relationship with God is our failure to accept the fact that we are stewards or trustees of our own lives—we fail to recognise our full responsibility to God and His creation ...

CHAPTER THIRTEEN

Wealth, The Challenge

I have always believed that leadership for a Christian is not optional, but mandatory.

As I pointed out earlier, we are called light, that we might lead the way. We are called salt, that we might penetrate everything and give it flavour. I believe Christians are "born again" to lead at every level of society. This brings me now to the challenge— The Four Questions To Achieve Greatness.

Some years ago there was a young man in our church called Gary, who looked and performed like a leader. Both he and his wife went overseas, and when they returned, Gary was sloppy, indecisive and lacking in motivation. I was concerned, as I was always on the lookout for leaders, and here before me was a young man bending under pressure and deserting leadership. I decided to tackle Gary on the problem. My wife advised me to take it easy on the young man, so I spent the next couple of weeks in prayer before speaking with him.

One day, at the end of a Sunday service, I caught Gary sunning himself outside against the church wall. I asked him if he would allow me to be involved in his life. He agreed, and I said first, "Gary, I want to ask you four questions."

"What age have you set for yourself to reach your full potential, that God might maximise your life?" was my first question.

Gary was visibly stunned, and shook his head. He said: "I've no idea, Mr. Daniels. Can I have the next question?"

"Right. Could you tell me in fifty pages or more what your full potential is in every area of your life?"

Gary shook his head again and said he couldn't because he had never thought about it. "Can I have the third question?"

"Gary, accepting that your full potential is one hundred per cent, what percentage rating would you give yourself right now?"

"A maximum of twenty per cent," he replied.

We chatted a little longer and then I walked off.

"Just a minute, Mr. Daniels," Gary called out. "Please give me the fourth question."

"Gary, you aren't ready for it," I called back and drove home. When I got home he was already on the phone, asking again for that fourth question. I reiterated that he did not need the final question because he could not answer the other three.

"Mr. Daniels, I have been praying a great deal about my future. I believe your questions, which were very timely, were an answer to prayer. Would you please give me that final question?"

So I asked him the final question; "Accepting the deficiency between the two scores, what plans are you going to make to take up the shortfall, and when?"

Gary wrote the questions down and, when I met him a fortnight later, he said he had spent a great deal of time laboring over them. With a group of friends he had sat up until the early hours of the morning, endeavouring to answer them.

I have since shared those questions with others, including business and church leaders and, in some cases, world leaders. One particular world leader has a specially embossed list of them on his presidential office wall.

Let us look at them and relate them to the pursuit of wealth as a Christian.

Question 1—What age have you set for yourself to reach your full potential that God might maximise your life?

When you consider putting an age on your full potential, all kinds of divisive thoughts spring to mind. The most obvious is: "How am I expected to know at what age I will reach my full potential?" The answer is, "You don't know". But you can set a target because God has given you the authority to do so through free will. Modern science has given great new insights into the mind—one of those is that the imagination is more powerful than the will. Take note here of the scriptural challenge of "as a man thinketh in his heart, so is he".

While it is true that your potential will expand as time progresses, so that in time you may want to change your selected date, this first question is not asked for that purpose. It is asking you to *forget* your limitations, ignore time restraints, and forget the other three questions. Come to grips with the great gift called life, and make a decision!

Firstly, forget obstacles. Allow your imagination to release itself from the bondage of present circumstances, restraints and self-imposed limitations. Spend a day coming to grips with freeing yourself! Accept now that God wants only the best for you and you do not need that excess baggage which is limiting you.

Secondly, recognise that your potential is there, and ready to unfold in any number of directions. Remember, the only limiting factors are the laws of God and those you put on yourself. Consider at what age you would like to see your full potential (as you perceive that potential now) realised. Ask this question continually until you feel in your inner being that quiet confidence that the decision you have made is comfortable. What I am really asking you to do relates to faith, because we cannot substantiate the decision with proof.

Having made the decision in respect to the age of reaching your full potential (taking care not to be influenced by the other three questions), consider your willingness to maximise your life's output within the boundaries of God's will and for His glory.

By the way, I am not going to spend time on the subject of God's will for your life, because I feel sufficient has been written by others to confuse the matter already! But I will express my own belief that God's will is first that none should perish. So a good starting point is to be involved actively in winning people to Jesus Christ. From then on, we should never violate the rights of man or the law of God, and from that point onwards, measure everything against the Word of God, and keep on striving, growing and giving.

The partnership between God and man is as old as creation itself. That He owns the cattle on a thousand hills and the wealth buried in every mine, illustrates His ultimate power and authority over our lives. It is obvious to me that what is lacking in our relationship with God is our failure to accept the fact that we are stewards or trustees of our own lives—we fail to recognise our full responsibility to God and His Creation.

With that in mind, we should consider that the problems of defeat, failure, poverty and suffering are not because of His lack of involvement, but because of our lack of involvement.

I have often heard the comment made when referring to another's mishap or misfortune: "Maybe you are running ahead of God." I believe that comment shows a lack of deep thought. Is it possible to beat God in our race to achieve? If we do presume to be in front of God, does it mean we are on the right track, but moving faster than He would like us to? I think the answer is "No" to both questions. But if you disagree, then ask yourself this question: If you are on the right track, would God not want you to go as far as you could and as quickly as you could? In other words, is it possible to run the race of life too fast while in the will of God? I think not.

To put off answering this first question is akin to enslaving your life to other people and circumstances, and ignoring God's greatest and most powerful gift to you—the power of *choice*. Adam had this power and he allowed circumstances to dictate his life's role. You have the same power in this age to make a choice. If you do not make a decision on this first question before moving on, you have effectively nullified your future achievement quotient.

And remember this, if you talk to others about it and let them influence you, you have destroyed your personal accountability and motivation—your responsibility is not at risk.

Question 2—Could you tell me in fifty pages or more, what your full potential is in every area of your life?

This second question invites you to get serious about your life. It invites you to stop being a surface-scratcher and encourages you to evaluate that marvellous gift of potential with a view to responding to the Giver by utilising your potential and power. It is amazing how few people actually *plan* any area of their lives—they get along by going along. The fact is, that we are mainly under-achievers in relation to our potential. The question may be asked as to *why* we should strive and achieve? After all, if we coast along as we wish, that is surely a matter of personal choice?

For the Christian, this is totally unacceptable. We were told before the Fall that we should work, tending God's garden, using our capacity to the full. After the Fall, this was emphasised even more. We also have been told to subdue the earth, to have dominion over it and to love our neighbours as ourselves. I believe this infers we are not to be a burden on our neighbours.

The attitude of some Christians that achievement is wrong, growth is wrong, and wealth of any kind is wrong, is comfortable, but terribly erroneous. That is because it immediately lets them off the hook as far as life's performance is concerned. We must understand the basic principle that if we do not achieve, we will have nothing to contribute to those less fortunate. And the potential is *known* to be here within us now. Physicians tell us we only use a small part of the brain's capacity and that we have enormous physical reserves. The Bible tells us that we also have inexhaustible spiritual reserves. We must conclude that there is nothing capricious in God's creation. He did not put potential there to be wasted, but rather to be used to glorify Him. So, let us look at our potential. *Firstly,* write out a resumé of who you are—a description of all your hidden talents. Do this in a conversational form. *Secondly,* divide your life up into sections covering spiritual, physical, mental, family and finance, and add any other items you consider important. *Thirdly,* turn on your dream machine and crystallise just what your greatest potential is in every area of your life, accepting before God that the reality lies within you and is anxiously awaiting release. Be honest, but be positive, and remember that even in your wildest dreams you could *never* outdream what God has in store for you.

My guess is that you will need more than fifty pages, and I suggest you write it in a lined book and date it—because it may be the *greatest single written document you have ever been involved with in your life.* You may think this is not for you. My reply is, "Then learn to fail gracefully." I say that, because anything that is not put in writing, will not be clearly crystallised in thought, and will therefore be limited in its scope and quality.

Read it often, but only make amendments after great consideration. The reason is that it will never have the same faith and substance the second time around.

Accept that you are a person of enormous power. Realise it does not come from you but *through you* from the hand and heart of God.

Question 3—Accepting your full potential as 100%, what percentage rating would you give yourself right now?

Approach this question not in the negative, but as if you were preparing for a long, interesting journey.

Observe the necessary tools and supplies you would need to reach your highest aspirations and goals, and prepare a shopping list. In this list there will be certain requirements which you already have at hand, for example, good health and a determined will. You may also have achieved certain academic levels and be geographically placed to your advantage. You may, in addition, have married and have a grown up family (look upon this as an advantage). These attributes are called *assets* and contribute significantly to your position.

Get excited about this part of your programme because you are now going to prepare a list of all the new habits—those that will motivate and discipline you in pursuit of your goals. Put a percentage mark on the personal equipment you have and the personal equipment you lack against an overall score of 100 per cent. Do not worry, even if your present position rates only five per cent, for this is your launching pad for dynamic assertion and long term motivation, which will provoke and propel you every day.

Look upon this stage—or this question—as putting you on the map of life, the starting point from which we plot our course to our final destination. But during your personal rating, keep in mind that you must be realistic, particularly in the area of suffering. Once, when I was asked if I could give one attribute for success, I said it was *the willingness to bear pain*. You are going to have to forego certain personal—sometimes intangible—comforts in favour of pain and disappointment, pressure and loneliness.

Looking at your percentage rating in this area, analyse it with *prayerful insight*. Do not blame others for your inabilities to handle pain. But do remember your inabilities can be handled by you if you are prepared to give them the attention they need.

Examine carefully any academic achievements you have made. But be very careful to put these in the correct ratings context. My view is that "professional students" as I call them, are those who spend a large part of their lives training for life's tasks. The real achievers have already *become* part of the action. A degree or doctorate is just a starting point and should never be a final goal. You must be results-oriented in the human arena and the scoreboard must be real, not imaginary, with the goals high enough to recognise a total result.

The percentage rating you have today will be different next year because of your involvement and dedication which will continue throughout your life. Remember, too, that your percentage margin may even become wider when you start to realise what opportunities are available.

In the previous question you had the opportunity to respond in respect to your full potential. The next question is not as heady or as edifying because of the reality of your present position.

Question 4—Accepting the deficiency between your two scores, what plans are you going to make to take up the shortfall and when?

You are now ready to move into top gear as you consider this last question. You have calculated the difference between the two scores and used that difference as a motivator for calculated action. Now come to the final thrust. Plans to achieve *must* be personal, otherwise they lack personal accountability and the thrust is destroyed.

The simplicity of making plans (or goals) to deadlines is often overlooked through a lack of the technical knowledge required. A simple method is to start at the grass roots level. Estimate your life's span. Exclude accidents but include your hereditary background and personal habits (smoking, drinking, etc.). It would be a good idea here to add the biblical truths relating to longevity. After estimating your maximum life span, bear in mind that a magnificent obsession to *achieve* can very often extend that period ten years or more!

The next step is to set your life's goals within that time frame. Some may find it difficult to accept life's goals, but the evidence for goal setting can be justified scripturally. And remember if you do not plan for life, you are going to do things by circumstances instead of by prayerful, planned consent.

If you have come with me this far in the book, then you have accepted that for the Christian, leadership is mandatory, and to ignore a plan after accepting it is tantamount to leadership suicide.

Now work back from your expected age and set timetables for each item, carefully allowing time for the things you enjoy and for family involvement. I have always maintained that the role of the busy, and often frustrated, executive, is usually a reflection of bad planning, bad habits and bad attitude.

Let me state clearly at this point: your family and church responsibility are part of your plan, not to be added in, but an *integral* part of the cement that binds it together.

Make deadlines on home and church commitments and relationships. Develop what I call *habit force* and never let an exception occur. Once you develop deadlines and meet them, then your personal self worth has a ring of integrity about it. I even go to the point where I read out an affirmation every day of who I am and what my responsibilities are before God. I ask what I am doing on this earth, and what I am going to achieve before my 80th birthday.

I write a letter to myself every month, telling myself how I am progressing in relation to my life's goals. I then take the letter I wrote a year earlier to find whether I had deceived myself.

I measure every working day, giving myself a possible score of 100 points. It is divided into areas, as follows:

AREA 1—Simplicity.

I give myself 25 points for simplicity—in other words, did I keep my day simple? This covers four practical areas—

1. *Organisation*—Was I organised for the day and throughout the day or did I allow circumstances, events or other people to reprogramme my day?
2. *Habits*—Were my habits controlled and in keeping with my goals or habits, or did I break down in any area?
3. *Clarity*—Did I have clarity in what I was about, or was I confused or frustrated?
4. *Assessment*—Did I allow space for myself for recon-

struction and assessment and prevent everything landing on top of me all at once?

Of course, simplicity goes much deeper outside of my daily plan and my whole life structure. For instance, I only own one pair of dress shoes. I always have black and I accept that I can only wear one pair at a time, so why do I need two pairs? I also go through my clothes wardrobe every twelve weeks and anything I have not worn, I give away. I keep very few extras and when I travel, I have it all down to a briefcase for a two week visit, which I carry on the plane. Keep life simple. Do not get hung up with gadgets and superfluous material items that take up your time, your space and your attention.

AREA 2—Desperation Quotient.

In this area I allocate 25 points for the desperation quotient of my life for each working day. I am a desperate man and I want to maintain that desperation till the day that God takes me home. I believe that if we were desperate enough, we would achieve more spiritually and commercially. That means a move sometimes into the pain zone area and it hurts, but you can increase your tolerance ratio as you exercise it. My desperation quotient covers four main areas—

1. *Intensity*—I need to pay attention to detail.
2. *Urgency*—Everything in which I am involved must give some credence to the speed in which the goal is going to be reached.
3. *Commitment*—The effort required to get a particular commitment fulfilled.
4. *Sacrifice*—There is no such thing as something for nothing. If you are going to do something in one direction, you have to let go of something else in another direction. You can only handle a certain amount at a time, which means that you must have courage and that courage means the courage to

give up as well as to take in.

AREA 3 Planning.

I give myself 25 points per day on my planning life. When I talk about planning, I talk about it in many different areas and the first one is life.

1. *Life*—In other words, the whole life plan that I have until my 80th birthday. This means that I have to watch out for milestones, so that I can monitor that life plan.
2. *Structure*—There must be segmentation right through the whole structure. It has to be broken up, so that I can handle it correctly.
3. *Feedback*—I have to be curious in whatever I am doing to give the feedback to make sure that I am on course with my planning and that the planning is accurate and true.
4. *Daily planning*—I need to have partitioning in all the other areas that I mention within this daily score, to evaluate what I am doing.

AREA 4 Action.

I also give myself 25 points on this. It covers four simple points under action. They are—

1. *Routine*—I have routine tasks to do every day and these must be done diligently and well and they are measured.
2. *Projects*—There are projects that I am involved with that require and demand my attention. These must not be let go, and I must monitor them regularly.
3. *People*—You cannot do anything without people. You must be involved with people. You have to be involved with people continually and I have to relate to them and I put a measurement on my relationship with people and how I can expand my people power.
4. *Profits*—It is no good working on activity, without objectivity. The object of running a business is to

provide a service and make a profit. I monitor my profits daily, so that I can assess each day whether I have made profits and thereby give my 1 to 25 point score.

If you meet me in the street any time and come up and ask me, what sort of a day I have had, I will open my diary and give you a score from 1 to 100 to tell you, with some accuracy, how my life is progressing.

I believe that every potential leader must learn to do something similar. Wealth leadership—and every other kind of leadership—presents a challenge. We are stewards and trustees of our lives, and as such, we are required to be found faithful (1 Corinthians 4:1,2).

Are you a faithful steward of your life for God today?

WHERE ARE THE LEADERS?

Where are the leaders, the guardians,
the guides, the pioneers?
Are they hiding, dead, or not to be found,
or are there none who care?

The need is great, the cause is true,
the battle line is drawn;
the ranks stay for a champion,
but none will face the dawn.

Must we perish in confusion,
put down, no more to rise?
Is there not just one deliverer
who will answer to our cries?

I sought from east to west, and then,
I sought from north to south,
to find a willing soldier
who would break the courage drought.

Perhaps a bugle call will rouse
the red blood in his veins?
Come quickly, bugler, sound the cry
to launch a new campaign.

The danger presses closer yet,
at every halting breath,
Arise and lead, please, someone,
before there's nothing left!

But not a murmur do I hear,
no single sound or call.
Perhaps I have to take the role
of leader, after all?

Then I'll do my best to lead the rest,
to danger I will go,
with muscles tense and iron will,
to charge against the foe.

With victory within our sight,
the enemy will flee!
And none will know until that hour,
that the leader could be me!

Peter Daniels